T0137621

PRINCIPLES
OF
ENTREPRENEURSHIP

PRINCIPLES OF ENTREPRENEURSHIP

Building a Resilient Windsor-Essex Economy
One Entrepreneur at a Time

Fabio Costante

Trafford Publishing

Trafford rev. 10/10/2011

 www.trafford.com

North America & international
toll-free: 1 888 232 4444 (USA & Canada)
phone: 250 383 6864 ♦ fax: 812 355 4082

SECTION I

People First

This book is dedicated to the residents of Windsor-Essex whose resilience knows no bounds.

Acknowledgements

This book owes its existence to many people including my influential university professors, entrepreneurs and everyone who helped edit and format the book.

A special thanks to my assistant Mohammad Yahya who worked tirelessly to help with the finishing touches, ranging from formatting to editing the content and photographs.

As in most of my work, I have been greatly assisted in many ways by my family and friends.

CONTENTS

INTRODUCTION

The "Principles of Entrepreneurship" is a book designed to help and assist first-time entrepreneurs and small-to-medium size business owners (SME's) in preventing mistakes and mitigating risks that are inherent in every business endeavor.

The guiding principles found in this book are derived and synthesized from a culmination of academic textbooks, journals, papers, case studies and through personal experiences of entrepreneurs, including the author.

The book outlines the lifecycle of a business and the important principles to follow and be aware of throughout. It will be laid out chronologically from defining what it means to be an entrepreneur to formulating an exit strategy for your business. Finally, it ends by illustrating how the role of the entrepreneur in society can stretch far beyond the buying and selling of goods and services in our economy.

The Windsor-Essex region is going through an unprecedented structural transformation that requires us to diversify our economy and build an infrastructure – an economy – that is far more resilient. Fostering entrepreneurship is one step in that direction.

CHAPTER 1

The Entrepreneur

To some people, the entrepreneur is one who is opportunity-obsessed, constantly seeking new ventures where profit can be realized (Timmons and Spinelli, 2004). It is also believed that the entrepreneur is cunning, ruthless and deeply ingrained in the greed that clouds their world. Entrepreneurs are thought to strongly believe that success is measured by income and is the determining factor for growth and progress.

Conversely, entrepreneurs are seen as artists who are inspired by the challenges of building great businesses. They have the ability to see an opportunity and act upon it, with the sole focus on building an empire. Money, to these classified entrepreneurs, is not of primary concern. In fact, money is only viewed upon as a tool to help build the business, analogous to the tools that are needed to construct a house or building.

Either description of the entrepreneur is valid and is commonly understood by many. However, these descriptions and other preconceived variations are limiting and may not be representative of the true dynamic of these individuals. Before learning the principles of entrepreneurship, it is necessary to have a better grasp of the entrepreneur by illustrating their distinct abilities and defining their roles.

Entrepreneurs are opportunity seeking and resourceful individuals with an uncanny ability to develop organizations around a common purpose – to sell a product or service that benefits a segment of the market that they serve. They are leaders in their own unique way and take a holistic approach in their methods of developing and growing their businesses (Bygrave, 1997).

Successful entrepreneurs have precious talents and abilities which include:

- Thinking big and 'outside the box'
- Understanding and fully capturing the reality of growth
- Enticing investment in all forms
- Persuading other talented individuals to participate in the common vision (Timmons and Spinelli, 2004)

Aside from these key attributes, what is certain of almost every entrepreneur is that their motivation and ambition is a distinctive characteristic that drives them continuously (Shaver, 1995).

Nature vs. Nurture

An ongoing debate is whether an entrepreneur is one who is 'born' or 'made' through the environment they perceive. Being a 'born entrepreneur' is difficult to judge and there is nothing that biologically proves or disproves such a theory; however, since attitudes and interpersonal skills can be developed and consequently contribute to the creation of an organization, entrepreneurs – and their encapsulated vision of the world – can very well be 'made' through time (Shaver, 1995).

There have been many instances where one grows up in a family of entrepreneurs and small business owners. To this person, starting a business is a normal and preferable way of life. The risk associated with developing and launching a business is perceived to be lower relative to what others may believe and the freedom of being 'the boss' greatly outweighs the rigidity of being an employee, irrespective of monetary and other material differences.

Throughout life, you learn and develop skills, whether it is through education (e.g. reading and writing), sports, work-related activities or certifications of some sort. Becoming a good entrepreneur also entails developing skills such as bootstrapping (discussed further in chapter 5), mitigating risk and perceiving it differently, managing growth, and building leadership abilities. In addition, you will pick up technical skills such as sales and financial expertise. Note that all of these aforementioned skills are transferrable and can be used in many capacities outside of entrepreneurship.

The skills that you learn can provide an avenue to entrepreneurship that allows you to fulfill your intrinsic and extrinsic needs. For some, entrepreneurship is about 'being the boss' and for others it is simply a 'good market opportunity.' Whichever reason you give, just keep in mind that being an entrepreneur – and a successful one – can be a developed trait and not necessarily something you are born to do.

Myths vs. Reality

There are common myths that surround entrepreneurship and cloud the true picture of reality. In Shaver's "The Entrepreneurial Personality Myth" the author outlines the difference between general perceptions of entrepreneurs and their reality (1995). They are outlined below.

Myth	Reality
1. Entrepreneurs need to own their business	• They do not need to own their business. Plenty of businesses are majority owned by investors and stakeholders and the entrepreneur simply focuses on building the business. Many entrepreneurs may prefer to bootstrap (discussed in chapter 5) their way to creating a product or service.

2. Entrepreneurs are immune to risk	• Successful entrepreneurs are not blind risk takers. The risks that they assume are carefully calculated and mitigated to a point where the decision to proceed (or not) is factored entirely.
3. Entrepreneurs are creative individuals	• Although many are creative, it is not a prerequisite to being a successful entrepreneur. In fact, many entrepreneurs launch a business that is not creative but through sheer execution intelligence and hard work, they become very successful.
4. Entrepreneurs are charismatic and extroverted	• This is not true of all entrepreneurs. Many are not charismatic and may even be introverted and shy.

What is certain of most entrepreneurs is their desire for accomplishment (Shaver, 1995). Their motivation and ambition are two key characteristics that enable them to work at levels desirable for success. They are tireless individuals, and need to be, if they dream of building a great business.

Many entrepreneurs succeed through an unrelenting conviction and persistence that drives them throughout their journeys. There is purpose to what they do along with tangible results of their potential and realized achievements. The fruits of their labour are explicitly apparent, consequently transforming entrepreneurship into a competitive game played between many players (competitors) and individuals. Ironically, sometimes the greatest challenge that they face is internal and lies within them: to constantly test their true potential and personal growth.

Common Characteristics

Research suggests some common trends in the characteristics that define successful entrepreneurs (Bhide, 1996; Timmons and Spinelli, 2004). These trends can be classified into four main characteristics that successful entrepreneurs possess and they include:

1. Being driven by goals:
   o Successful entrepreneurs most likely have an end goal in mind when pursuing their venture. Furthermore, they have short-term and long-term goals and objectives that are measurable and clearly attainable. These goals and objectives are of primary concern and their completion usually dictates the success of the business, especially ones that are time sensitive.

2. Enduring persistence and optimism:
   o Persistence, or even courage in some cases, may be the key factor in the success of a business. It is almost inevitable that the journey of entrepreneurship entails peaks and valleys where the key to survival may simply lie in the degree of persistence that an entrepreneur attains. Being able to see beyond the tragedies and bad times is a shared ability of successful entrepreneurs.

3. Good judgment
   o Relentless optimism and persistence combine to make a strong and sometimes dangerous mix for entrepreneurs. If entrepreneurs have a good sense of judgment, then these characteristics prevail. On the contrary, being overly persistent and blindly optimistic may cloud the entrepreneur's judgment to the point of irrational decision making.

4. Strong self-discipline
   o Finally, the last of the four common characteristics is having strong self-discipline. This is a characteristic that is programmed and learned through repetition

and habit. It is the effort made by the individual to work hard and effectively, despite all of the adversities, setbacks, achievements, and milestones.

Leaders

Entrepreneurs are leaders and must be so if they hope to succeed. They demonstrate good communication skills by persuading their team and company towards a unified vision. The best entrepreneurs can motivate their employees by incorporating a team culture where everyone is treated equally, with respect and dignity.

Leaders must make decisions daily and thus good judgment becomes an important factor. Always with the entity (the business) in mind, successful entrepreneurs make decisions – irrespective of their consequent popularity – that will benefit the organization that they lead. Once a decision is made, there is no looking back, unless of course, there is the luxury of time or resources to do so. In most cases, both resources and time are scarce and therefore every decision made must be executed properly. Mistakes are inevitable and will occur frequently; however, what is much worse than making mistakes is not making a decision. There typically is not much time to contemplate in the game of entrepreneurship. Thus, it is better to make a decision and contingency plan in case things go wrong as opposed to being indecisive and sitting on the fence for too long.

Although many entrepreneurs thrive on individual success and achievement, they are more concerned with the overall status of their business. For this reason, these types of entrepreneurs have an easier time attracting talented people and can build a solid team atmosphere. It takes a strong leader to recognize his or her weaknesses and thereby recruit people who have greater expertise or are simply better in other areas than them.

Lastly, the entrepreneurial leader must be action-oriented. They must lead by example and must be the hardest working individual in the business, at least in the startup phase. There is no exception here. If those who are following the leader see complacency or any sign of laziness, then they will become unmotivated and unproductive through time.

Entrepreneurs in Our Communities

Entrepreneurship can ultimately be defined in a myriad of ways. Truthfully, there is not one clear definition that encapsulates the entire meaning or practice of entrepreneurship, especially since entrepreneurship encompasses many different work-related fields in our communities.

Entrepreneurs come from all walks of life that transcend age, sex and race. Those under the age of 29 are categorized as 'youth entrepreneurs' and most are typically involved in small business ventures, ranging from the service sector (such as consulting) to owning a pub or perhaps launching a construction business, focusing on a specific trade. There are a few, however, who invent life changing products or services that either create new industries or completely revolutionize existing ones. Many of these types are found in the science labs, engineering faculties, or simply in the garage with a few friends who possess an infinite curiosity for making things better than their current state (The owner of facebook was in college working out of his student dormitory when he launched his venture).

It is also fair to assume that the young entrepreneurs tend to be the more creative type, adapting more easily to recent trends and educated under a new era of technology and innovation. Sometimes their creativity stems from simply being naive, in which ignorance truly is bliss. Without realizing the amount of effort and time needed to invest in order to become very successful, these entrepreneurs dive in head first into an uncertain journey and sometimes never look back.

There are other entrepreneurs who may be regarded as innovators – those concerned mainly with making things better, whether they produce better technology or simply make people's lives easier through some better mechanism. Their greatest motivation stems from the art of change. They could be scientists, engineers, physicists, or just an average citizen trying to make the world a better place.

In many cases, the greatest challenge to these entrepreneurs comes from commercializing their technology or great idea. Transforming an idea into an opportunity (to be further discussed in Chapter 3) is essential to the success of these entrepreneurs.

There are many entrepreneurs who have a deep social conscience and can be classified as 'social entrepreneurs.' They can be found in many places such as non-profit organizations, government and non-government institutions, universities, corporations, and small businesses. Although they have parallel mindsets to the typical entrepreneur mentioned at the beginning of the chapter, their focus is greatly inspired by helping people and society at large.

They may have founded food banks, environmental organizations, or homeless shelters – all with an innovative approach to using resources and ensuring sustainability within their respective organizations.

Another dynamic group in Canada is the new immigrants that come year-after-year and who, for many, partake in starting a small business. These 'immigrant entrepreneurs' (new Canadians) have the essential skills and abilities of domestic entrepreneurs, in addition to a different perspective and in many cases, access to different resources, mainly from their homeland. Their greatest asset is providing unique products or services to the country that they inhabit. These types, from research and through experience, are very hard working individuals who are relatively conservative in their management of risk and growth (Schlosser, Costante and Shallal, 2007).

Chapter 2

The Team

Many small businesses do not necessarily require a team to get launched; however, at some point, entrepreneurs recruit people for various reasons: to grow their business, alleviate work hours, or just rearrange priorities to other areas of their lives. This chapter presupposes that, if not at the startup phase, eventually you will need a team of people working in your business and thus it is important that you recruit the right people who can make your business better and help you achieve your vision.

Recruiting a team may refer to attracting a partner, a manager, an employee, or even a part-time helper. All of these people are instrumental to the success of your business and thus should be recruited cautiously and prudently. Moreover, it is important to recruit people when needed, not just when desired. There ultimately must be purpose as to why one is recruited to your business.

The old adage of 'getting the right people on the ship' is fundamental to the overall success of the business. It is the job of the lead entrepreneur to develop a cohesive team where each member complements each other. The best entrepreneurs are able to attract talent without paying high compensation by selling the opportunity and 'big picture' (Timmons and Spinelli, 2004; Wasserman, 2008). This may imply giving up equity in the business or perhaps developing autonomous roles where the members function as a team, as opposed to subordinates.

After conducting countless interviews and through personal experience, it is clear that one of the biggest challenges of building a great business is finding the right people to steer the ship. It is extremely difficult to convince highly talented individuals to take a risk and live without secure pay – even if only for a period of time. Nevertheless, it is possible and although the process of finding the right people is challenging and time consuming, the long-term benefits will greatly outweigh the short-term delays.

Look for Winners

Some of the characteristics that define a winner include persistence, perseverance, discipline, strong work-ethic, resilience and the desire to achieve and grow personally. You can find winners everywhere. They do not need to possess fancy degrees or have a wealth of experience. They are the people who always strive to be the best at what they do; whether that mean's being the best teacher, factory employee, sports coach, etc.

Winners are people in your community who make their workplace and environment better because they have learned how to learn and work well in the field they are in with the characteristics mentioned above. Such winners tend to be rewarded with company incentives such as 'employee of the month/year' and many are recognized throughout their communities for the work they do. Look for these winners when building your team.

Filling the Gaps

When building the right team it is important to first understand your strengths and equally as important your weaknesses. Once you truly understand both, you will have an idea of where you need the greatest help and expertise. Thereafter, you are able to scout for talent that will compensate for your weaknesses and thus fill the necessary gaps in the team.

Too many times, entrepreneurs hire and attract like-minded people due to environmental attraction or interpersonal bonding. For example, engineers may attract their engineer friends or financiers may attract people they work within the finance industry. Although these people may be well qualified and able, it does not necessarily mean the team as a whole will function optimally, consequently impeding on the maximum potential of the business.

Moreover, attracting similar minds may hinder decision making and ultimately produce a dogmatic vision in the company. Therefore, it would be advisable to seek talent that is different than yours. This gives your team myriad perspectives and the business benefits from extracting various expertise and knowledge.

Having the right mix of talent and deploying team members to their relevant positions allows them to be accountable to their role. Furthermore, it gives each individual more responsibility in their work – a feature all winners seek; both the former and latter work in favour of the entrepreneur and the team.

The Illusion of Total Ownership

The perception of being the boss and therefore having complete control has hindered the performance and execution of countless businesses (Wasserman, 2008). Entrepreneurs who attract the right people should not worry about giving up ownership. Furthermore, in order to attract the right talent and expertise, giving up ownership is oftentimes encouraged. Thus, the entrepreneur must always ask the fundamental question: what is better for the business, having a large piece of a small pie or a small piece of a very large pie? To those who are self-indulged or rather prefer to control as much of their business as possible, they choose the former. To others who prefer high growth, expansionary businesses, the latter is much more beneficial; especially when dealing with high growth businesses that demand the alleviation of control to prosper and attract talent.

Many regard this as profit sharing which becomes a very popular model when executed properly. This idea implies that the business is built on a promise of future growth and prosperity, resulting in a business with greater value where everyone gains. Most importantly, it allows entrepreneurs the tools they need to entice the best people possible without paying them a large salary. The very successful entrepreneurs have this candid ability. They are willing to give up equity in their business because they know it will ultimately assist in attracting talented teammates.

Experience

Experience may not be essential; however, the more experience one has in small business and entrepreneurship, the better and more able one can adapt to the environment and subsequently make fewer mistakes, particularly in the beginning.

Many entrepreneurs, when launching their business, have no experience whatsoever yet they are able to build and grow their business to millions, and in some cases billions in revenue. These entrepreneurs rely more on their intuition and gut – without discounting calculated and objective thinking – to make decisions. They most likely do not make repeat mistakes or in other words, they only make new mistakes in what is referred to as 'failing forward.'

There is, however, one area where past experience could very much help determine future success and that is if two or more entrepreneurs have previously worked together and were successful, in any capacity. In this case, if two people respect each other as people and colleagues – and are able to separate the two when necessary – then that may be enough evidence to predict a successful partnership and team going forward.

Finally, an important subset of the experience factor lies in the social capital of each member and team as a whole. As entrepreneurs recruit talent, they should keep in mind the people who they are recruiting and perhaps just as important, how well these people are connected. An example may be hiring an individual who worked in a similar industry to your business, knowing that they have access to key networks and resources, their social capital becomes very important and perhaps even essential.

Family & Friends Paradox

How many times do we hear stories where brothers, cousins, parents and children, or close friends get in disputes and before you know it, they're suing each other in court over breach of contract or other illegal activity? This is what we call the Family and Friends Paradox, where family and friends – those who are generally closest to you and who therefore you think you can trust – surprisingly deceive, steal, or manipulate to their advantage.

It is because you blindly trust these people and would never expect any wrongdoing from them, that you become less cautious and could be more vulnerable to deception. Let us be clear, not all family and friends will betray you, nor do they have any intentions of doing so. In fact, there are many successful family businesses. Of these, there is one common trait: the family and/or friends are able to clearly separate business from personal life.

Above all, if you can avoid bringing in family and friends to the business, then it would be wise to do so. It is imperative that a business be managed as a business and not a family gathering where you sell a product or service. Quite frankly, successful businesses have demonstrated historically that they do not work this way and there is a greater risk of failure due to emotions prevailing over rationale and objective business decision making.

Section II

Identifying an Opportunity

CHAPTER 3

Idea into Opportunity

Entrepreneurs typically discover an idea by experiencing or noticing a flaw, inefficiency, or discomfort in a product, market, or process (Fry and Killing, 2000). The expression 'entrepreneurship is born on a bed of pain' is widely cited and reflects how ideas are generated; however, these ideas are not all good opportunities.

To know whether your idea is a good opportunity, you must first do some research in five areas that explicitly demonstrate the validity of the business (Fry and Killing, 2000; Timmons and Spinelli, 2004). These include:

1. The market
2. The economics of the business
3. The competitive advantage and strategic differentiation
4. The management team and its fit with the business
5. Harvesting issues

As we approach these characteristics in greater detail, you will understand why many ideas oftentimes do not get very far.

The Market

The first question that you must ask yourself when launching a business is "What market are you serving?" Are you focusing on age groups? Sex? Race? Geography? Once you can answer these questions, you can subsequently research the dynamics of the market.

This consists of another subset of questions which include:

- Is the market growing or shrinking?
- Are there niches within the market? If so, can you serve one in particular?
- Are customers easily reachable?
- Is your product or service needed in the market and how does it ultimately benefit the consumer?
- What is the average income level of your customer?

Entrepreneurs tend to be over-ambitious. They believe that they can serve many aspects of a market simultaneously from the day they launch their business. Being the 'jack of all trades and master of none' is very dangerous, especially when your resources are limited and your brand is yet to be established.

The best advice for first-time entrepreneurs is to find a niche in the market and to serve it well. A niche is a segment of the market that is underserved or overlooked. A market niche may consist of offering a complementary product or service that is unique, serving a specific demographic, or offering a specific service to fill a demand in the market.

Become an expert and fully immerse your business in that niche. Once you master a part of the market, it becomes much easier to grow and expand. Your business is then creating real value and building a recognizable brand (Bhide, 1996).

Furthermore, with a focused niche, you are able to concentrate your marketing efforts on one particular market segment. This allows for better and more effective marketing where you will get the most value for dollar spent.

Observe, research, and learn your marketplace. By doing this, you set the foundation for building a good business and although the process is meticulous, you will discover many things about the market and more importantly, about your own business.

Gathering the right information may entail literally visiting the market. For example, if you intend on providing a product for teenagers, it may be wise to schedule focus groups or provide seminars where you can receive feedback on the product. Use your creativity and think of ways to reach out to your potential market.

Some ways to seek information may come from the internet, books, statistics, market studies, newspapers and universities. Another effective way to gather information is simply conversing and gathering input from industry and trade contacts.

The Economics of the Business

When you launch a business, it is inevitable that most of your time will be dedicated to it if you want it to succeed. Since this is a given, wouldn't it be wise to launch a business that makes healthy profits and provides solid growth? If the answer is yes, then by all means, think big!

Before you decide to launch your business, it is wise to formulate projecting financial statements (ProForma). These give you an idea of the potential of the business in terms of revenues, costs and profits. Do not take the optimistic approach when making these financial statements. In fact, being a bit pessimistic may help you prepare for turbulent situations and give you a better perspective of the viability of the business. Wishful thinking is common across entrepreneurs who oftentimes tend to be overly optimistic. Thus, it is probably best to get various perspectives from qualified people on your financial statements.

If you find it difficult constructing the financial statements, you should seek an accountant or a consultant who may be able to assist you and simultaneously give an objective viewpoint. This gives more credibility to the business and may encourage or discourage its continuance.

Here are some key financial measurements you can use as a benchmark in knowing if the economics of the business are appropriate (Fry and Killing, 2000; Timmons and Spinelli, 2004):

- A minimum of 40% gross margins (difference between revenues and costs of goods sold)
- Strong cash flow (a measurement of how much cash enters and exits your business continuously)
- Recurring revenues
- Low assets
- Good working capital (your ability to pay short-term debts with relatively liquid assets)
- Profit potential of 10% to 15%

Not all of the above must be met in order for your business to succeed. Also, consider that the ProForma is speculative and you will most likely not achieve the numbers that you project, whether you perform under or over the benchmark figures (Sahlman, 1997). The ProForma does, however, provide a guide for your business that changes as your business evolves. Therefore, it should be flexible enough to allow for such unforeseeable changes. In other words, if you are entirely dependent on your projected numbers just to survive, then your business is most likely not a good opportunity.

The Competitive Advantage and Strategic Differentiation

Assess the factors that make your business competitive by completely understanding the internal and external forces that drive your business. Can you be the lowest cost provider and if so, how? Is your product or service truly different and better for the consumer? Do you have relative control of the processes and structures in your industry by ways of exclusive agreements or patent controls? (Timmons and Spinelli, 2004)

If you can answer yes to at least one of the three questions above, then you may have a real competitive advantage and are able to create value in your business.

With respect to strategic differentiation, you want to look for fluid integration and fit within your internal resources – people, assets and capital – and your overall strategy. You also need to assess the relationship between your business and the external environment, to demonstrate how your strategy uniquely fits with the environment to realize opportunities (Fry and Killing, 2000).

The Team and its Fit with the Business

When the team has a proven track record in the industry, along with trust for each other and integrity, then opportunities become much more attractive for all stakeholders. Furthermore, when the team's goals and values coincide with the business, there is much promise in its success.

For any business, the team (or entrepreneur) must be ready and willing to devote most of their time and energy, in addition to dealing with high stress environments. Thus, if the team is right for the business, the opportunities could be endless.

The team plays a deciding factor in determining the opportunity of the business. Please refer back to Chapter 2 for more detail on constructing the right team for your business.

Harvesting Issue

Entrepreneurs presuppose that the exit strategy – when and how they will sell their business – is probably the last thing to consider when deciding whether their idea is an opportunity. This is false. Knowing your exit mechanism is just as important as the other criteria already described. Even if you do not intend to sell your business in the near future, it will eventually have to be sold, divested, liquidated, or transferred somehow. Knowing this, you should always plan ahead and look at the feasibility of harvesting (selling) successfully.

If your business can create real value through processes, technology or other competitive advantages, then the exit strategy becomes much more attractive and attainable. Conversely, if your business provides no different value from your competitors and is simply a price taker – a homogeneous business that mainly survives by extracting what is left in the market – then you will have trouble harvesting and this makes your idea less of an opportunity.

Contextual Factors

In addition to the five criteria above, there are also contextual factors that play a major role in determining the richness and feasibility of the opportunity (Fry and Killing, 2000; Timmons and Spinelli, 2004). Some of these may include:

- Changes in the regulatory environment
- Industry dynamics changing and breakthroughs occurring
- Globalization and the implications involved
- Societal changes

Do any of the above affect your business? How? Is your business dependent on any of the above? Is your business flexible enough to adapt to its environment?

All of these questions should be asked when assessing the context with which your business is associated.

It is clear that simply thinking of an idea and implementing it without doing your homework is unwise. Also, following the information provided in this chapter does not completely guarantee your idea will be a good opportunity; however, it will mitigate the risk and uncertainty to a point where you can make better decisions – meaning you could take a more calculated risk and not just a blind one.

Section III

Managing Resources

Chapter 4

Raising Capital

Finding adequate financing, from all available sources, is one of the most important functions of an entrepreneur. A new business faces many challenges in raising capital which brings forth three fundamental questions (Dollinger, 2003; Timmons and Spinelli, 2004):

- How much money should you raise before starting the venture?
- What type of investor should you approach for the venture?
- What is a better method of financing – equity or debt?

This chapter will help explain these three common questions with which entrepreneurs are faced everyday and give you insight into the art of entrepreneurial financing.

Deciding How Much Money is Needed

Before discussing the amount of money one should raise to start a business, it must be emphasized that money should not be the first priority. Very often, entrepreneurs focus on just raising money when that should not be the primary and sole focus of the entrepreneur or team. This is because of a cause and effect relationship between the opportunity (the business idea) and capital (debt/equity). In other words, money follows opportunity and thus a business should focus on the opportunity (the cause) and money should thereafter come rolling in (the effect).

The issue of how much capital to raise becomes very tricky because raising insufficient funds may seriously damage the new venture in times when the business is under cash constraints (undercapitalized). Conversely, raising too much cash may cause the new venture to be overcapitalized and inefficient.

Not raising enough capital could potentially cause your business disappear before it ever truly takes off. This is because, typically, a new venture burns cash before it has the ability to build cash (positive cash flow). In this case, if too little is raised and the entrepreneur does not know how much cash the business can use before going bankrupt, then serious problems will occur inevitably.

Conversely, when the entrepreneur raises too much cash, issues may arise such as (Bhide, 1992; Gompers, 2002):

- Sending the wrong information to stakeholders
- Unnecessary spending and inefficiencies
- Excess cash earning low returns, which diminishes total return on investment (ROI)
- Giving up too much equity (financial ownership of the company) because early capital is most expensive since you have yet to create significant value in the business

It is clearly evident that the amount of capital to raise is extremely crucial to success. A new business should always focus on their cash flow and how much money they will use before getting out of the 'red' and becoming profitable. Therefore, staged financing – raising capital as the business goes through its lifecycle – is the best approach, if done correctly (Timmons and Spinelli, 2004).

Staged financing allows an investor to minimize risk while providing the entrepreneurs with just enough capital to be efficient and focused. Every unique business needs different capital infusions at different times. What is most important is that you know your business, its lifecycle, and the timing of cash flows.

Choosing the Right Investor

When deciding on the appropriate investor for your business, you must understand what type of business you are running and which types of investors are drawn to certain business criteria. The economics of your business (Discussed in detail in Chapter 3) are integral to deciding which investor or lender must be sought.

If you are starting a business that produces high margins, high growth, and a strong cash flow, you may be qualified to look into angel investors (wealthy individuals who invest in private businesses and usually mentor the entrepreneur or team) or venture capitalists (investors that manage assets of private companies and typically seek high returns in a 3 to 5 year time-span). Although both angels and venture capitalists (VC's) are mainly private equity investors – and may require a large equity stake in your company – you may benefit greatly from having them on board. Aside from the necessary capital, they also provide expertise, guidance, and a vast array of networks that can help your business grow and alleviate risk.

If, on the other hand, you are starting a business that produces the opposite as the aforementioned criteria – such as a restaurant, retail shop, or any other type of small business – then you probably will have more success searching for other sources of financing, primarily debt from banks and lending institutions. These types of institutions typically require collateral or other forms of protection, which deny many entrepreneurs from realizing their dreams. If you do not have any substantial personal assets, such as a house, then you should look for a private investor – family, friends and acquaintances – who may be interested in your idea but always keep in mind the family/friends paradox discussed back in Chapter 2.

Whichever method you choose should always be contingent on the type of business you are leading and the amount of capital you require.

The Type of Financing for Your Business

Now you must decide which method of financing between debt and equity is best for your business. Again, this is completely dependent on the nature and stage of the business. Equity financing basically means giving up a percentage of your company in return for money and expertise. Equity investors include angel investors, wealthy individuals and venture capitalists should you have the appropriate type of business.

Sources of debt financing may be suitable for businesses that have plenty of hard assets and collateral to leverage. Debt investors include commercial bank financing, line of credit loans, accounts receivable financing, time-sales financing, unsecured term loans and trade credit. There may be other methods that suit your unique business, but the aforementioned are the most common.

Here are some quick tips for choosing between debt and equity financing (Timmons and Spinelli, 2004):

For debt:

- Borrow when you need it
- Read each loan covenant (agreement) and requirement carefully
- Be conservative and prudent

For equity:

- Ask three central questions
  1. Does the venture need outside equity capital? Could the business manage without it?
  2. Do the founders (entrepreneur or team) want outside equity capital?
  3. Who should invest?

One very important factor to consider when shopping for capital is the macro-environment. Being in an economic recession or boom may greatly impact the chances of accessing capital and the price you pay for it.

Always remember, money follows opportunity and good opportunities should always be the primary focus of the entrepreneur. Raising capital should never be the greatest obstacle if your opportunity is feasible and credible.

Chapter 5

Bootstrapping

We learned in chapter 4 that you should focus more time on building a great business and naturally, money will follow. Entrepreneurs waste an inordinate amount of time searching for cash when they do not need to. The art of bootstrapping – doing as much as you can with as little as possible – is what usually separates successful entrepreneurs and businesses from average or unsuccessful ones.

Bootstrapping Resources

When assessing your resources – people, assets (plant and equipment) and money (debt or equity) – you want to ensure that you use them wisely – enough to fulfill every stage of your business lifecycle, without affecting your overall business.

The odds of receiving funding from private investors are extremely low, even harder when you have little experience and credibility. The fact is that the majority of entrepreneurs fund their businesses through their personal savings, credit cards, 2nd mortgages and so on (Bhide, 1992). This is the rule, not the exception. Furthermore, most businesses are not going to be financed by a venture capital firm (VC's) or by angel investors. Remember, the type of financing you choose must fit your overall business model and strategy. Angels and VC's typically want to cash out with high returns – more aggressively with VC's than Angels – and that may not reflect the long term strategy of your business. Also, investors may impede on a business' flexibility in the early stages because they believe that their initial plan must be rigidly followed through.

Bootstrapping is a wonderful thing for entrepreneurs as it allows them to see all the flaws inherent in their business. As opposed to simply throwing money at problems which induce inefficient business practices, a business that bootstraps well can fix the underlying issues in many businesses and thereby create a more sustainable, healthy business.

Bootstrapping Strategies for Your Business

Bootstrapping, in a sense, is very instinctual. It transcends across business and even personal life. Simply put, bootstrapping allows you to see the world differently and encourages you to focus on the important things in life and business. It constantly reminds you what it is you are doing and why you are doing it. It requires having a keen focus on being efficient and the ability to alleviate the costs of doing business as much as possible, without harming the strategy and business model. Some strategies to employ early on to assist in bootstrapping your business include (Bhide, 1992):

- Beginning operations as quickly as possible; starting small and focusing on sales
- Looking for quick, break-even projects in the early stages
- Offering products or services of value where customers do not need to be persuaded by expensive marketing campaigns. Personal selling and passion will be vital in achieving your goals and objectives
- Focusing on building a good, strong team with an emphasis on attracting winners
- Expanding only at the rate you can afford
- Prudent focus on cash above profits and market share. Cash will later finance your growth and provide a healthy working capital. "Cash is king!"
- Renting instead of buying for any physical assets

There are infinite amount of ways to bootstrap your business. Always ask yourself the simple question: How can I do more with less? This principle will allow you to progress in your business while simultaneously exposing both your strengths and weaknesses.

Doing more with less and using your resources efficiently will take time and practice. There will be mistakes and many setbacks and it will be an ongoing, continuous process. Keep in mind that your business will never be perfect. You will never be perfect. But striving for perfection is what drives people and businesses. It is what motivates you to get up early in the morning and stay late at night. The idea of perfection and the intricate rigor in trying to achieve it can put you on the journey to success.

Control vs. Ownership

Just because you control your resources, does not necessarily mean you must own them, and vice versa. Entrepreneurs who bootstrap effectively are able to control their resources without owning them. An example may be leading your team without paying them a salary, but rather sharing the equity of the business and subsequent profits with them. Other examples include renting space and equipment, borrowing money from institutions or people or extracting as much relevant information through cost-efficient sources such as the internet and other related materials instead of hiring expensive consultants.

Free yourself from the thinking that you need to own everything in order to be successful. Trust, in business and especially in the startup phase, prevails over all other theories and methods. Without trust, it will be difficult to succeed. You must have trust in the people facilitating your resources and they must be able to trust you and your business.

Section IV

The Entity is First Priority

CHAPTER 6

Managing Growth and Scaling Up

In the world of competition, you are either growing or you are dying. There is no such thing as stagnation. Once you reach the growth stage of your business lifecycle, there will be some very difficult decisions to make. Always keep in mind one important question as you experience this phase: What is in the best interest of the business entity? If you can constantly ask yourself that question and execute based on the related solutions, then you should be able to successfully manage the growth stage.

The transition from starting a business and then managing its growth is quite substantial. The qualities required for the early stages change throughout the lifecycle and if the entrepreneur is unable to adapt accordingly, then it may severely impede the overall success of the business. Let us look at some examples of challenges that may occur during the growth stage.

Blind Loyalty to the Team and Employees

Blind loyalty can hinder the management of a growing, more complex business (Hamm, 2002). When leaders fail to see weaknesses and gaps, they put the business at risk. As the business grows, leadership becomes much more important and must grow accordingly.

Do not confuse loyalty with blind loyalty. Loyalty between people is what every organization should have; however, blind loyalty – which assumes the person is doing their job effectively with no basis to support your claim – is a dangerous conception. Always assess your team and employees objectively and make sure they are ready for the growth phase, assuming you are as well.

Too Focused on the Small Things

As your business begins to grow, the small tasks that are usually consumed in the operations of the business and were once important end up becoming a heavy burden on your time (Hamm, 2002). Thus, entrepreneurs and leaders must find ways to streamline their operations and strategy, focusing on the big picture while developing priorities for key strategic initiatives.

Excessive attention to the small tasks will hinder your abilities to think big and subsequently manage growth. Micromanaging, as an example, becomes far too costly and so there must be a transition from managing employees to managing managers. Such transition entails alleviating much control. It requires greater trust and will ultimately be best for the business and the people that work in it.

Too Narrow and Insulated

As the business expands, so should your mind. Tunnel vision is dangerous. A single-minded leader who does not communicate nor listen to employees may lose them entirely. Every leader should foster unique and different input from their employees, especially during the growth phase. Their insight is always valuable and should be taken seriously.

It is disastrous to see leaders work in insulation when their business is heavily reliant upon customers, investors and other key stakeholders. The notion that entrepreneurs work alone is a myth. There are many days where the job of the leader is very lonely but this does not discount the importance of communication, trust and respect with all the relevant internal and external parties of the business.

Misunderstanding Your Core Strategy

Your market niche may need to change or expand during the growth phase. This becomes tricky because it may feel appropriate to diversify the business but getting into unrelated projects may ultimately spread the core business too thin. Therefore, a united strategy that does not stretch your resources too thin, irrespective of how well you can bootstrap or even how much money you can raise from investors, must be in place.

Other issues occur in the ever-changing and dynamic relationship between your suppliers and customers. This interrelates with understanding what it is that your business does and the role your stakeholders play in it. Always re-examine your business model and have a good understanding of the purpose that you serve in the marketplace (Timmons and Spinelli, 2004).

Mismanaging Operations

The biggest and most detrimental flaw entrepreneurs make while managing operations in the growth phase occurs in their inability to properly manage working capital. Oftentimes they over-extend their credit, become excessively leveraged, or poorly track their pricing and costs. This is why raising capital (Chapter 4) and bootstrapping (Chapter 5) should be taken seriously if you wish to manage growth successfully and not end your business in bankruptcy.

Working capital is essentially the ability to pay your short-term loans (current liabilities) with your most liquid assets, referred to as current assets. This is why it is important to have a healthy amount of cash and timely account receivables to ensure such payments. This is one reason why cash flow is more important than net profits.

It is clear that your business may experience its main challenges in people, strategy and operations during the growth phase. Therefore, entrepreneurs must develop new ways of getting work done and thereafter institutionalize these methods. Going back to the very basics, let us identify how you can cope with growth through a series of reflective questions and solutions.

Growth Strategy

How will your business grow? Will it grow through new customer segments, new geographic markets, or new products/services? Once you know how, you then must ask why? Does the new growth model fit with your core strategy? (Hamermesh, Heskett and Roberts, 2005).

People

Before your roles were informal and flexible, now they become more rigid and narrowly defined. Can your employees and team cope with this? Can you? Perhaps it may be time to reconsider roles, if necessary, including your own (Hamermesh, Heskett and Roberts, 2005).

Opportunity

The greatest opportunities in the growth phase occur through the choices of the growth strategy. Thus, it is advisable to assess your strategy meticulously and, equally as important, to understand the fit between your strategy and your business model. Always keep in mind that the goal is long-term sustainability (Hamermesh, Heskett and Roberts, 2005).

Context

Changes in the economy (capital markets) may affect your strategy and must always be taken into consideration. During recessions, it is much more difficult to access capital and thus it becomes increasingly more challenging to manage growth. If you are ready to grow, always develop a contingency plan and understand your environment, the competition, the industry, and the economy. This may have a large effect on how aggressively you can grow and expand (Hamermesh, Heskett and Roberts, 2005).

Given the complexities of staged financing and knowing when to seek capital, it may be time to bring in a seasoned, professional Chief Financial Officer (CFO) to the business. This is one who thoroughly knows the game of entrepreneurial finance and is able to get the best deal possible, given the contextual circumstances.

As you can see, it is fairly difficult to manage growth as new challenges arise, some which are out of your realm of expertise or are unmanageable, given the resources you have. It is wise to always ask the question that was posed at the beginning of this chapter: What is in the best interest of the business entity? Using this question as your guide, you will be able to move your business forward even if it entails selfless motives or major personal sacrifices.

Chapter 7

Exit Strategy

According to the Canadian Federation of Independent Business (CFIB), approximately 71% of entrepreneurs intend to sell their businesses over the next 5 to 10 years. However, only 10% of these entrepreneurs have a formal succession plan (Quoted from ProfitGuide. com: The Trillion Dollar Trap, 2006)

Defining and outlining an exit strategy should always be on the mind of the entrepreneur. It is an ongoing process that should be planned before the business is launched because it helps guide the business in creating value. Entrepreneurs should set timelines of when they want to exit their business and maintain a solid vision throughout the lifecycle of the business. They should constantly be monitoring the market to benchmark their business against others.

Planning Ahead

It is important to plan from the very beginning so that when it comes time to sell your business, you are getting the most value for your hard work. Ways in which you could plan include:

- Setting personal goals and objectives from the launching phase of the business
- Understanding the full implications of decisions you make and their relationship to your exit strategy

- Constantly monitoring opportunities to sell, such as when your business has reached its maximum value – normally after the growth phase of your business lifecycle
- Seek alignment amongst team members and employees

Never underestimate the importance of planning your exit strategy. Although it may seem overzealous, prudent planning will ultimately be beneficial. Moreover, it is wise to plan an exit strategy before you launch because that may persuade or perhaps even dissuade you from starting the business. A sound exit strategy is a key factor in determining the holistic opportunity of the business.

The Two Most Common Exit Strategies

Although there are myriad of ways to exit from your business, the two most common methods used by entrepreneurs in the small-to-medium size business sector include (Petty, 1997; Timons and Spinelli, 2004):

1. Strategic acquisition
2. Outright sale

The strategic acquisition option is when the small business, or an agent, identifies competitors in the industry who would benefit from acquiring their company. In other words, synergies could be realized after the acquisition is complete. For these synergies to be realized, it is imperative that the acquisition makes business sense. Thus, acquirers may look at important elements such as:

- Intellectual capital
- Geographic scope
- Clientele base
- Complementing product line
- Core competencies (your business strengths)
- Vertical or horizontal integration (where and how synergies will be formed)

These are only a few, among many, reasons for a company to acquire or merge with another.

An outright sale is another very common route that entrepreneurs take when looking to harvest their business. These sales are typically targeted to wealthy individuals, investors, aspiring entrepreneurs, venture capital firms (for high growth ventures), and any other individual or group interested in purchasing the business.

Prior to the acquisition or sale, there has to be a common agreement as to the valuation of the business which includes both qualitative and quantitative factors that determine value. Here are some critical drivers when valuing a business (Timmons and Spinelli, 2004):

1. Qualitative Factors
   a. Customer loyalty
   b. Relationship with suppliers, buyers and other key stakeholders
   c. Brand recognition
   d. Niche market strategy
   e. Breadth and/or depth of products and services
   f. Competitive advantage
   g. Strategic differentiation

2. Quantitative Factors
   a. Good cash flow
   b. Healthy working capital
   c. Strong financial ratio's
   d. Recurring revenues from existing customers
   e. Revenue growth
   f. Good margins
   g. Earnings Before Interest, Taxes,
   h. Depreciation and Amortization (EBITDA)
   i. Efficient turnover

It is so important to plan your exit strategy from the beginning mainly because of the various factors that must be considered. Such factors, both qualitative and quantitative, should be questioned and assessed constantly from the day you start your business to the day you sell it.

Other Exit Strategies

Other exit strategies for entrepreneurs of small businesses include management buy-outs (MBO) and cash flow realignment (Petty, 1997; Timons and Spinelli, 2004).

An MBO is when the entrepreneur simply sells the business to management, either in the form of cash or stock, and sometimes in combination of these two. A cash flow realignment, on the other hand, is when an entrepreneur either funds new businesses out of the excess cash of the current business or increases their personal cash flow by only keeping enough funds for operating needs.

Emotional Attachment

It is common for entrepreneurs to be emotionally attached to their business; after all, it is their creation. For many entrepreneurs, the idea of exiting from their business is frightening but, irrespective of age, if the entrepreneur is focused on what's best for the business, then eventually at some point, he or she should exit with a clear mind and purpose as to why and when the business is for sale.

When coming up with a fair valuation, the entrepreneur must think objectively and not let emotions take over. In other words, the entrepreneur must not let personal beliefs inflate the price and value of the business. This is why it is usually best to get a 3rd party perspective when deciding to sell. A business valuator, accountant, or consultant should be able to give a fair valuation and different perspective into the business.

As previously mentioned, there are many unique ways to form an exit strategy. If the planning and monitoring take place early on in the business, entrepreneurs have a better chance of meeting their exit strategy. Too often, entrepreneurs, who work endless hours on their business, end up selling for a lower price because of ineffective planning. Do not make this mistake, remember to always plan ahead.

Section V

The 21st Century Entrepreneur

CHAPTER 8

Value Driven Entrepreneurship: A Baker's Story

The entrepreneur, knowing or not, implicitly plays an important role in the economy, this is clear and unequivocal. Although most entrepreneurs are focused solely on their business, perhaps there is a larger purpose for what they do that extends further than just the market that they serve. Under the premise that we are all subjects of society, it is always beneficial to think beyond oneself and look at how you can impact your local community. This requires an assessment of your personal values and aligning those values with a purpose to serve those who are most vulnerable.

I once lectured at a cross-border seminar, promoting entrepreneurship as one of the solutions to the local region's economic problems. After the series of lectures, I was fortunate to have mingled with local citizens and community leaders. There, I was passed on a piece of wisdom that has stuck with me ever since. One individual said, "I really enjoyed the lecture and believe what you said will be valuable for any entrepreneur; however, there is one thing I think was missing from the presentation." At this point, he had the attention of a small group of us as he continued: "You see, I was hoping to learn more about what happens after you become a successful entrepreneur. Then what? Aside from creating a product or service for a particular market, what happens after?"

At first, I was confused. The question he posed was outside the scope of what I was lecturing about. But as time went on, I kept thinking about that question and then began to realize that perhaps there is a wider, more meaningful reason to engage in entrepreneurship that is beyond the notion of just serving a particular market with a product or service. Perhaps there is something greater than the individual achievement or the business itself. A higher purpose! Then it dawned upon me that recreating and rethinking an entrepreneur's role in society may be a vital step forward for economic and social justice.

The Baker

At the age of 33, a gentleman by the name of Orlando Greco was heading to a small village in the south of Calabria, Italy – approximately 25 minutes from his home – to look for work. Ideally, he wanted to open and manage a bakery in the town for three main reasons: 1) He had past experience working in the bakery business; 2) He was good at the profession; and 3) He truly loved it.

Through his social network, he was able to pitch his idea to a fairly wealthy individual who had previously known about Orlando's work. After negotiating a wage and free rent, the two men teamed up and opened a bakery. Within months, the bakery was picking up business and building recognition across the small Italian village. Then came the turning point, where they received an order to supply bread to a local village nearby. "The business was exploding," he claimed as he recalled buying another bread-baking machine and subsequently hiring 7 employees.

There were two main reasons why he was doing well: 1) The quality of bread was unambiguously of better quality than the competition and 2) He did much more than just make and sell bread to the village people. The former is self-explainable; the latter alludes precisely to what the individual was asking me, "What happens after?"

Orlando was loved by the village people. He was a giving man and his relationship with the village people was symbiotic in that sense. As an example, he would give bread to the poor for free or at minimum, for high discounted prices. Of course, he would not make this public nor use it as a public relations strategy. Conversely, he would make sure no one knew but the people receiving the kind gesture and him. He understood the poor folks would be embarrassed and denigrated if others found out, especially in such a small village where he worked. In response for his giving, people would return him gifts – of no great material value but sentimental, nevertheless – and would love and respect him for his generosity.

At some point, there was news spreading that he was giving bread away for free to poor people. When Orlando found this out, he quickly arranged a meeting with his staff (team) and immediately knew at least one of the employees – without knowing who – was responsible for spreading such news. Thereafter, he gave them an ultimatum that either the person(s) confess and they apologize publicly to the families who were derided after the news spread, or, he furiously said "either I quit or fire all 7 of you and hire 7 new employees tomorrow."

Eventually one confessed and later quit because he was too ashamed of what he had done. This is just one small illustration of Orlando's grand character. He led through his values and always shared whatever he had with those less fortunate.

In addition to helping out as many poor people as he could, he also respected everyone with common courtesy. Another example is when he would make 20 pizzas on the odd occasion and personally deliver them to people all throughout the village, again, free of charge. Ultimately, he knew it was the right thing to do and I am sure it was good for business too.

By doing all these great deeds, he made many friends and alliances in the village. From the local police and mayor, to the poor people and farmers, they all loved him. "Those were the greatest years of my youth," he exclaimed with a sense of nostalgia. Later in his life, he decided to immigrate to Canada mainly for better opportunities for his children and grandchildren, again, for selfless reasons.

I could find no better way to articulate the main point of this chapter – leading through your values – than portraying the entrepreneurial venture Orlando presided over. It was personally touching to hear this story and the timing could not have been better (coincidentally, this story was told to me at the same time I was trying to figure out how I was going to write this last chapter of the book).

The holistic role of the entrepreneur is now crystal clear. Whether you can donate money (profits) to some charity or cause, or simply give people free bread, there is much more to the entrepreneur than the traditional buying and selling of goods and services, and it starts and ends with your values – what you believe to be right and just.

Here was a man who was adored by almost all of the people in his village and he was only a baker, a man with no great sum of money or clout. Orlando Greco, my grandfather, has taught me that dedicating your life (career) to something greater than yourself has no minimum standard. Anyone could make even a small difference in the lives of others. You are all powerful and influential in your own unique way and if you dare to achieve greatness, let it not be solely measured by material gains but rather in the subtle ways you can contribute to the common good, the greater good.

ABOUT THE AUTHOR

Community volunteer, entrepreneur, published author and a leader who is dedicated to public service — these are just a few of the phrases that have been used to describe Fabio Costante.

In 2006, Fabio founded and was President of Students In Free Enterprise (SIFE Windsor) – a non-profit organization committed to creating economic opportunities for residents of Windsor-Essex through entrepreneurship and self-employment. The organization is currently in its 6th year of operation and has over 50 members.

Fabio has held various managerial professions in both the non-profit and private sector and has been consulting for small-to-medium sized businesses for several years.

As a community volunteer, Fabio has been actively involved in Windsor's west-end community where he has organized various neighbourhoods and engaged citizens through the ourwestend.com blog.

Fabio also served as Co-Chair of Pathway To Potential – Windsor and Essex County's poverty reduction strategy. He was co-chair of the roundtable, the steering committee and also chaired the jobs and employment working group. Pathway To Potential is a multi-sector collaborative that includes the business community, non-profit, all three levels of government and individuals with lived experience.

Fabio attended Francis Marion University on a soccer scholarship and received an Honours degree in Business and Economics as well as a Master of Business Administration (M.B.A.) degree from the University of Windsor.

Fabio is currently enrolled in law school, studying both at the University of Detroit Mercy School of Law and the University of Windsor School of Law, and anticipates to graduate with a Juris Doctor (J.D.) degree by 2013.

Bibliography

Bhide, A. *The questions every entrepreneur must answer.* Boston: Harvard Business Review, 1996.

Bhide, A. *Bootstrap Finance: The Art of Start-ups.* Boston: Harvard Business Review, 1992.

Bygrave. *The Entrepreneurial Process.* New York: John Wiley & Sons, 1997.

Dollinger, Mark. *Entrepreneurship: Strategies and Resources.* Upper Saddle River: Prentice-Hall, 2003.

Fry, J.N. and J.P. Killing. *Strategic Analysis and Action (4th ed.).* Scarborough: Prentice-Hall, 2000.

Gompers, P.A. and W. Sahlman. *Entrepreneurial Finance.* Boston: Harvard Business School Press, 2002.

Hamm, J. *Why Entrepreneurs Don't Scale.* Boston: Harvard Business Review, 2002.

Hamermesh, R., JL Heskett and MJ Roberts. *A Note on Managing the Growing Venture.* Boston: Harvard Business School Press, 2005.

Hisrich, R.D. and M.P. Peters. *Entrepreneurship (5th ed.).* New York: McGraw-Hill Irwin, 2002

Petty, J. William and John D. Martin. *Financial Practices Among High-Growth Entrepreneurial Firms.* Babson College, 1997

Sahlman, W.A. *How to Write a Great Business Plan.* Boston: Harvard Business Review, 1997.

Shaver. K.G. *The entrepreneurial personality myth.* Business and Economic Review, Vol. 41 No.3, pp.20-3., 1995.

Schlosser, Costante and Shallal. *Barriers Facing Canadian Immigrant Small Business.* Windsor: University of Windsor, 2007.

Timmons, J.A. and S. Spinelli. *New Venture Creation (6th ed.).* New York: Irwin McGraw-Hill, 2004.

Wasserman, N. *The Founder's Dilemma.* Boston: Harvard Business Review, 2008

Glossary

Angel investors: An investor who provides financial backing for small startups or entrepreneurs. Angel investors are usually found among an entrepreneur's family and friends. The capital they provide can be a one-time injection of seed money or ongoing support to carry the company through difficult times.

Bankruptcy: A legal proceeding involving a person or business that is unable to repay outstanding debts. The bankruptcy process begins with a petition filed by the debtor (most common) or on behalf of creditors (less common). All of the debtor's assets are measured and evaluated, whereupon the assets are used to repay a portion of outstanding debt. Upon the successful completion of bankruptcy proceedings, the debtor is relieved of the debt obligations incurred prior to filing for bankruptcy.

Business Model: The plan implemented by a company to generate revenue and make a profit from operations. The model includes the components and functions of the business, as well as the revenues it generates and the expenses it incurs.

Business Valuation: The process of determining the economic value of a business or company. Business valuation can be used to determine the fair value of a business for a variety of reasons, including sale value, establishing partner ownership and divorce proceedings. Often times, owners will turn to professional business valuators for an objective estimate of the business value.

Capitalization: A modification in the issued and outstanding securities of a company. Capitalization changes occur either through the issuance of additional shares or the repurchase or cancellation of existing shares. This can have a dilutive or accretive effect on a company's market capitalization, depending on the scenario.

Cash burn: (Burn rate) The rate at which a new company uses up its venture capital to finance overhead before generating positive cash flow from operations. In other words, it's a measure of negative cash flow.

Cash build: (Emergency Fund) An account that is used to set aside funds to be used in an emergency, such as the loss of a job, an illness or a major expense. The purpose of the fund is to improve financial security by creating a safety net of funds that can be used to meet emergency expenses as well as reduce the need to use high interest debt, such as credit cards, as a last resort.

Core competencies: The main strengths or strategic advantages of a business. Core competencies are the combination of pooled knowledge and technical capacities that allow a business to be competitive in the marketplace. Theoretically, a core competency should allow a company to expand into new end markets as well as provide a significant benefit to customers. It should also be hard for competitors to replicate.

Current Assets: In personal finance, current assets are all assets that a person can readily convert to cash to pay outstanding debts and cover liabilities without having to sell fixed assets.

Collateral: Properties or assets that are offered to secure a loan or other credit. Collateral becomes subject to seizure on default.

Consultant (Investment Consultant): An advisor who helps investors with their long-term investment planning. An investment consultant, unlike a broker, does more in-depth work on formulating clients' investment strategies, helping them fulfill their needs and goals.

Debt: An amount of money borrowed by one party from another. Many corporations/individuals use debt as a method for making large purchases that they could not afford under normal circumstances. A debt arrangement gives the borrowing party permission to borrow money under the condition that it is to be paid back at a later date, usually with interest.

Equity: In terms of investment strategies, equity (stocks) is one of the principal asset classes. The other two are fixed-income (bonds) and cash/cash-equivalents. These are used in asset allocation planning to structure a desired risk and return profile for an investor's portfolio.

Feasibility (study): An analysis of the ability to complete a project successfully, taking into account legal, economic, technological, scheduling and other factors. Rather than just diving into a project and hoping for the best, a feasibility study allows project managers to investigate the possible negative and positive outcomes of a project before investing too much time and money.

Globalization: The tendency of investment funds and businesses to move beyond domestic and national markets to other markets around the globe, thereby increasing the interconnectedness of different markets. Globalization has had the effect of markedly increasing not only international trade, but also cultural exchange.

Horizontal Integration: When a company expands its business into different products that are similar to current lines.

Lender: Someone who makes funds available to another with the expectation that the funds will be repaid, plus any interest and/or fees. A lender can be an individual, or a public or private group. Lenders may provide funds for a variety of reasons, such as a mortgage, automobile loan or small business loan.

Liquid Assets: An asset that can be converted into cash quickly and with minimal impact to the price received. Liquid assets are generally regarded in the same light as cash because their prices are relatively stable when they are sold on the open market.

Macro Environment: The conditions that exist in the economy as a whole, rather than in a particular sector or region. In general, the macro environment will include trends in gross domestic product (GDP), inflation, employment, spending, and monetary and fiscal policy. The macro environment is closely linked to the general business cycle, as opposed to the performance of an individual business sector.

Margin: The amount of equity contributed by a customer as a percentage of the current market value of the securities held in a margin account; In a general business context, the difference between a product's (or service's) selling price and the cost of production.

Market Niche: A small but profitable segment of a market suitable for focused attention by a marketer. Market niches do not exist by themselves, but are created by identifying needs or wants that are not being addressed by competitors, and by offering products that satisfy them.

Marketing Campaign: Specific activities designed to promote a product, service or business. A marketing campaign is a coordinated series of steps that can include promotion of a product through different mediums (television, radio, print, online) using a variety of different types of advertisements. The campaign doesn't have to rely solely on advertising, and can also include demonstrations, word of mouth and other interactive techniques.

Mortgage: A debt instrument that is secured by the collateral of specified real estate property and that the borrower is obliged to pay back with a predetermined set of payments. Mortgages are used by individuals and businesses to make large purchases of real estate without paying the entire value of the purchase up front.

Patent: A government license that gives the holder exclusive rights to a process, design or new invention for a designated period of time. Applications for patents are usually handled by a government agency. In the U.S. the United States Patent and Trademark Office handles application and documentation.

Price taker: A firm that can alter its rate of production and sales without significantly affecting the market price of its product.

ProForma Financial Statements: Pro forma financial statements could be designed to reflect a proposed change, such as a merger or acquisition, or to emphasize certain figures when a company issues an earnings announcement to the public.

Recession: A significant decline in activity across the economy, lasting longer than a few months. It is visible in industrial production, employment, real income and wholesale-retail trade. The technical indicator of a recession is two consecutive quarters of negative economic growth as measured by a country's gross domestic product (GDP); although the National Bureau of Economic Research (NBER) does not necessarily need to see this occur to call a recession.

Recurring Revenue: The portion of a company's revenue that is highly likely to continue in the future. This is revenue that is predictable, stable and can be counted on in the future with a high degree of certainty.

Segment: A component of a business that is or will generate revenues and costs related to operations. Financial information should be available for a segment's activities and performance and must also be periodically reviewed by the company's management before a decision can be made regarding the amount of capital that will be given to the segment for a particular operating period.

Short term debt: An account shown in the current liabilities portion of a company's balance sheet. This account is comprised of any debt incurred by a company that is due within one year. The debt in this account is usually made up of short-term bank loans taken out by a company.

Social capital: An economic idea that refers to the connections between individuals and entities that can be economically valuable. Social networks that include people who trust and assist each other can be a powerful asset. These relationships between individuals and firms can lead to a state in which each will think of the other when something needs to be done. Along with economic capital, social capital is a valuable mechanism in economic growth.

Stakeholder: One who has a share or an interest in an enterprise. Stakeholders in a company may include shareholders, directors, management, suppliers, government, employees, and the community.

Startup: A company that is in the first stage of its operations. These companies are often initially bank rolled by their entrepreneurial founders as they attempt to capitalize on developing a product or service for which they believe there is a demand. Due to limited revenue or high costs, most of these small scale operations are not sustainable in the long term without additional funding from venture capitalists.

Venture Capitalist: An investor who either provides capital to startup ventures or supports small companies that wish to expand but do not have access to public funding.

Vertical integration: When a company expands its business into areas that are at different points of the same production path.

Working capital: A measure of both a company's efficiency and its short-term financial health. The working capital ratio is calculated as; Working Capital= Current Assets − Current Liabilities Positive working capital means that the company is able to pay off its short-term liabilities. Negative working capital means that a company currently is unable to meet its short-term liabilities with its current assets (cash, accounts receivable and inventory).